Stop
the
Spinning

Move from Surviving to Thriving

LAURA GISBORNE

ISBN: 146998122X

ISBN-13: 9781469981222

Library of Congress Control Number: 2012901787

CreateSpace, North Charleston, SC

ACKNOWLEDGEMENTS

I know that I would not be here today if I had not been blessed with some amazing people in my life. My journey did not start out easily, but there have been people who have loved me and "seen" me when I could not see myself. I am writing this book as a thank you to those people, including the following:

Barbara Wiesinger, for providing a safe home for me as a child and continuing to love and support me as an adult. Estrella, for letting me know that life "did not have to be this way." Tom Norris, for showing me that a different world existed from that which I knew. Amy and Carlos Torre, for a lifetime of friendship and for being my family of choice.

My grandmother, Mildred Harrison, who I have had the privilege of knowing and loving in the past few years. Peter Seemann, for loving me when I could not love myself and for being a wonderful father to our two children. Susan Henkels, for always listening and never judging. Ellen Solart, for coming to me with my "Next Step." Elaine and Dean Edelson, for supporting me unconditionally on this journey of leadership when I did not have a clue on how to proceed. Jacob Seemann, for being such an amazing gift in my life and for hours of support, both emotionally and in the office. Erika Seemann, for being my best friend and the person who asks the tough questions.

A special thanks to my life partner and coadventurer, Scott Gisborne. I am in awe of your ability to stand strong in the face of adversity. I am honored that you have chosen me to explore and grow with you over these last twelve years. I love you very much and am so grateful to continue the journey with you.

INTRODUCTION

It is my hope that the experiences I share in this book give you inspiration to step into a life that is all that you want it to be. I am writing this book for anyone who has ever felt that they were "not enough." I have had the honor of meeting so many people who have shared their stories with me over the years, and I have attempted to address as many of the common themes I hear in their stories as I can by sharing my stories. It is my fondest wish that this book provides inspiration and motivation for you so that you too may live a full and joyful life. Each of the chapters represents a life lesson that has moved me from surviving to thriving. The first letter of each chapter's title is significant.

When you put them together, they spell the words POWER UP. It is my hope that you can embrace any or all of these principles as they may serve to empower you in your own life.

My first invitation to speak publicly came a few years ago. For many years, friends, peers, and psychics told me that I had a message to share, but I was not clear at all what that message was. I would frequently meet someone on a plane, or at one of the retail stores I owned and within a few minutes the person would open up like a fountain to share with me his or her deepest feelings and experiences. Often we both wept, and I was told, "I don't know why I am telling you this," or "I have never shared this with anyone before." I was never sure why this was happening or what I was supposed to do with it. I knew that something magical occurred frequently with complete strangers, and it felt like my "job" to be there and hold them safely.

When I was originally asked to speak to groups, I didn't put two and two together. Like many people who feel they are being "called," I questioned why I was being asked to serve, what I had to offer and, more importantly, how I could actually help others. I had very mixed emotions about moving out of my comfort zone and into my purpose.

Currently, I live a life that many people only dream of. I live in a large home that I designed and built with my husband in the "Country of the Country" in Cornville, Arizona, just outside of Sedona. Our beautiful property sits on the banks of Oak Creek surrounded by centuries-old sycamore trees, inside a private canyon, down a two-mile private dirt road. Our "front yard" is planted with merlot grapes. I am married to a gorgeous man who was completely taken aback when I said it was time for me to go out into the world and serve my people.

My life was not always like this. I was born in Pittsburgh, Pennsylvania, in 1966. That is almost all I know about my origins. In my earliest memories, I was living with my mother and stepfather in a small house in Kansas. My stepfather was in the military, so we moved frequently. I don't remember much about our family life in the early years, other than I knew early on to be seen and not heard. When I was almost five years old, my stepbrother was born, we moved to Florida, and I had a new purpose in life. My baby brother was so cute and tiny and I loved playing with him. My mother let us know frequently that she wished she had never had children and that she could have had a much better life if she weren't saddled with us. Most days when my mother came home from work, she drank herself to sleep on the couch. My brother and I spent our afternoons with our beloved babysitter, Barbara, and our evenings alone. My stepfather was rarely around, and if he was home, we did our best to stay out of his sight. Weekends were spent with Barbara, if she was able to keep us, or with friends of my parents who we called "Aunt and Uncle" though they were no relation to us. Our Aunt would take care of my little brother while our Uncle took me out. He told his wife we were going shopping, visiting the zoo, or riding horses. I don't recall where he actually took me, but it always included being molested in his car. When my brother and I spent the night at their house so my parents could have a break from us, I would go to sleep alone and wake up with my Uncle in my bed.

My stepfather was an angry man. We learned early on to adapt to his moods and addictions. Although many people say that marijuana is not addictive, my stepfather depended on it as his drug of choice. Years later, when my mother and he divorced and he became a violent alcoholic, we wished for the former addiction. If my stepfather was high when he got home from work, he would be the "happy" dad, and my brother and I had little to fear. If it was like most days, however, he would be coming down from being high and anything and anyone in his path was in trouble. My brother and I would cower in fear when we heard him coming into the house. My stepfather wore a large belt covered with holes and rivets that had a large metal buckle. It shook with a terrifying rattle when he took it off to "make an impression" on us. We tried to be quiet and good to avoid hearing the rattle of that belt being taken off.

As a teenager, I realized that I could get permission to be away from home frequently as long as I kept my straight "A" average and did the cleaning and chores necessary to make life easy for my parents when they got home from work. What I didn't realize was that my brother bore the brunt of my parents' emotional outbursts while I was gone. As a young teenager, I knew that I could stay out of trouble as long as I didn't rock the boat.

When I was seventeen my stepfather had an affair. I don't know the details of the relationship, but I do remember coming home one day and finding my mother holding a loaded gun to his head. They were both drunk at the time, and I wanted to get away from them, but more importantly, I wanted to keep my little brother out of the way. I am not proud to say that I didn't care too much about what they did to each other, but I realized that my brother had been in the middle of all of their chaos without any buffer since I had gone out and become a busy teenager.

The gun didn't go off. I managed to get myself and my brother out of the house, and when we returned home, it was like nothing had happened.

The ups and downs were frequent and dramatic. We grew up walking on eggshells and trying to stay out of the way. As a child and teen, I experienced a great deal of abuse - emotional, physical, and sexual. Today I realize that my parents did the best they could with the tools they had, but both were in pain themselves and heavily addicted to drugs and alcohol.

Someone who meets me today sees little evidence of the young woman I was twenty years ago. At twenty-one, I was severely anorexic and living with a man who beat me on a regular basis. I worked two to three jobs while putting myself through college. I was literally surviving day to day and didn't dare dream that life could be any different. My driven behavior masked an unacknowledged hope that maybe one day I would finally be "good enough." Like all of us, I only knew what I knew. We all do the best we can with the knowledge and experience we have. Thankfully, I quickly learned that my past didn't have to define my future.

I am so grateful for the mentors and angels that have come into my life. I am humbled by the fact that they could see me even when I could not see myself. I am also grateful for the people who showed me that life could be so much more than simply surviving.

My first husband was one of the first people who cared for and nurtured me. I grew tremendously during our time together. I was always a hard worker, and he and his family gave me opportunities and a focus for my energy. Since I started working, I had been a good employee, but having the opportunity to be a part of a family, along with being a part of a family business, rocketed my development. Everyone in the family worked very hard, strenuous hours, and we were all on a quest to grow and develop. My father-in-law was like the "Rich Dad" mentor to me that many have read about in Robert Kiyosaki's book, "Rich Dad, Poor Dad". He was a self-made success and he was brilliant and generous in sharing his knowledge with all of his kids – both his natural born children and those, like me, who he adopted.

I loved the opportunity to learn from my father-in-law, but after several years, I felt that there had to be more to life than work. Our entire family was incredibly committed and hard-working, and it appeared at times that nothing really mattered outside of the business. Since I had never had a close family relationship, I was grateful for the opportunity to work six to seven days per week, ten to twelve hours per day to be a part of something bigger than my meager self.

After several years of marriage, we had done very well financially. I realized that we were doing well professionally but our marriage and home life was not ideal. Through no fault of my husband, we had become efficient business partners, and good parents, but we had very little communication with each other as life partners. My husband and I tried some counseling, but nothing seemed to bring us back together. It was such a sad time for both of us, as we had a tremendous amount of respect for each other, and were filled with hopes and dreams for our futures going into the marriage. After our big move to Sedona, we had a painful year of growing. I was offered a sales job and took to my new opportunity like a duck to water. My husband committed to caring for our young children while I worked and did not find any easy work opportunities in our small, rural town. I was thriving in sales, but held little compassion or empathy for my husband staying home with our children. This is a time of my life that I am not proud of. My husband was doing his best, but I was only focused on work and our young children. The man I loved, who had given me his all, became invisible to me. I was only interested in my own growth and our children. We eventually agreed to divorce.

Divorce was a great wake-up call for me. I couldn't understand how I could be doing so well professionally and yet suffering so much personally. I was so busy making a living that I was not in tune with what was truly important to me. I had to take a step back and say to myself, "This is my wake-up call. If I want to move forward from this point, things are not going to be the way I thought they were going to be. What would I like my life to look like from now into the future, and what must I do to make this happen?"

Learning to let go of the things that don't serve you is a tough battle sometimes. Learning to let go of the people who are not in alignment with your goals and values is even tougher. Oftentimes we have people in our lives because we feel that we should or ought to, but those very same people do nothing but keep us from focusing on and achieving our goals. This is hard to look at, but everyone must. How are you going to improve the way you feel about yourself and the way you see the world if you continue to surround yourself with people who pull you down? You won't.

Establishing boundaries with people who are not in alignment with your goals and values doesn't mean you can't have them in your life. You may, however, choose not to live with or work with these people on a daily basis. Letting go of people you care about is especially hard, but you must learn to not allow others' opinions to influence how you feel about yourself. Learning to structure your life around the people who support you, both personally and professionally, sometimes requires tough decisions.

Do you feel sometimes like you have to do everything for everybody else? Often we feel like we have to serve everyone around us to the point that we're not serving ourselves. We must learn to honor our own needs. We have to become clear about our time and how important that time is!

Spend some time, whether you do it while you are reading this book or in the near future, pondering what you want the next year to look like. Take responsibility for what is coming next. Look at yourself honestly and ask, "What do I want the coming year to look like?" If you don't make life better for yourself, who will do it for you? Take action now to create the life that you love and allow success to happen for you. This first small step will help you to be open to your future teachers and mentors when they come to you. It is time for you to surround yourself with the right people, and let go of the ones who may care for you, but whose actions or beliefs are not supporting you in being all you can be.

CHAPTER ONE

The Power of One Minute

"How you spend your time is how you spend your life."
Laura Gisborne

We all know only what we know. We experience the world through a filter of our experiences and current knowledge. Have you ever looked back at something that you experienced five or ten years ago and realized that it would appear very differently to you if you experienced it today? Often the experiences that are so painful when we are going through them, give us strength and insight for our future journeys.

Many of the people I meet around the world operate on some type of autopilot. Some strive to grow as children and young adults, but then settle into their lives when they get comfortable and stop looking for opportunities to grow and learn. Their lives appear to be working just fine for them, until one day they have an experience that shakes them to their core. It is what I refer to as "wake-up calls." Wakeup calls can come in many forms, but for most they seem to happen in one of three ways - I call them the three D's: Death, Disease, and Divorce. These seem to be the points in peoples' lives when they realize that what they have been doing hasn't been working. These wake-up calls provide the impetus to look at life a little differently. For some, it is the first time in their lives that they become aware of their mortality and time suddenly becomes important.

The first "D" is Death. Experiencing the death of a loved one reminds us not only of our own mortality, but often brings up regrets. We consider everything that we would have liked to have said or done with a person that we no longer have the opportunity to be with anymore. Time has slipped away.

The second "D" is Disease. When we, or someone we love, experience a life-threatening illness, the world seems to stop. Our time becomes truly limited, and we must consider what we want to experience or achieve in the time we have left. What will forever remain undone?

The third "D" is Divorce. This can be a literal divorce—the end of a marriage—or the dissolution of a significant relationship. Relationships act like a mirror for us. We get to see ourselves in a whole new way when we see how we relate to others. Without being aware of what is happening, we feel that we are complete when we see ourselves reflected back through a relationship. When that reflection no longer exists, we are often left feeling incomplete and begin questioning ourselves and our lives.

Clients often seek me out to work with them on creating business systems and structures to increase productivity. Every single one of them to date has had a challenge around his or her relationship to time. This relationship is the most significant game changer for people, both personally and professionally, that I have ever witnessed.

In my twenties and early thirties, I was the poster child for the slogan "I don't have time." It didn't matter who asked me to do something or what they wanted me to do, this was my pat response. I had moved from where I was doing everything I could for anyone and everyone to the opposite end of the spectrum. I became so busy making a living and being self-important that I was completely unconscious in my day-to-day living.

Getting divorced showed me how just how self-involved I had become. With two small children at home, I was forced to slow down and take a look at my world. I adored my children, but I did not adore the woman I had become.

I slowly became aware of how much pain I had caused myself and others by not being present. By not valuing myself and the relationships I had been gifted, I ended up losing time that could never be recovered. I finally began to get clear on the gift of time and how precious it actually is.

All human beings have exactly the same amount of time on a day-to-day basis. Some live longer or shorter lives, but most people experience the same

essential structure of twenty-four hours in a day
and seven days in a week.

One of the biggest mistakes in life that people
make is not honoring their time. Amazing people
who create amazing lives - Gandhi, Martin Luther
King, Nelson Mandela - all shared the same
timeframe that you and I do: twenty-four hours
in a day, seven days in a week. The difference is
clearly how they chose to spend their time. Most
people are completely unaware of how they spend
their time. Without some sort of structure, time
keeps ticking away.

People who are successful in their lives honor their
time and clearly understand that it is a deeply
important commodity. People tend to view money
as a commodity, but in my opinion time is the only
true commodity. We are born and we die. While
we are living, the time between these two events
is continuously diminishing. When you clearly
understand the value of your time, and become
aware of how you are spending it, the world
suddenly appears as a different place.

I would like to suggest an exercise that my clients
find very revealing. Find a timer you can set for

one minute. (You can find one on the web at www.Stopwatch.com, if you don't have one readily available.) Close your eyes, take a deep breath, get comfortable in your chair, and simply be with yourself for one minute. You don't have to do anything. There's nothing you need to do or be or see right now. Sit quietly for one full minute, please.

Many people are preoccupied with their seeming lack of time. What did you experience when being still for one minute? For me, it always feels like a long time. One quiet, still minute is really a pregnant opportunity. After you become fully aware of the power of one minute, you realize that there are sixty of those in every hour and twenty-four hours in every day. A lack of time is often the first excuse I hear from people about why they cannot live a life that they love. Once we realize that we all have the same amount of time, we can choose to view this differently.

The second excuse is money. (We will dive deeper into this topic in the next chapter.) Write down everything that you would do and be if you had all the time in the world and all the resources. If time and money were no longer excuses for you not to live a life that you truly love, what would your life look like? This exercise might take a few minutes, but it is worth completing. The purpose of this book is to move you away from living on autopilot to living a life that you love.

When I did this exercise for myself several years ago, I discovered was that my desires fell into categories that were at two ends of the spectrum of possibility. Some felt really easy to achieve, though I had labeled them as not possible or practical due to my lack of time. I discovered that if I had free time, I would like to spend it hiking with my children, reading, exercising, and learning how to play piano.

At the opposite end of the spectrum, I listed bigger and more unattainable goals. I would travel to Africa, Australia and New Zealand. I would make a significant impact in my community to support women and children.

This exercise revealed many places in my life where I was playing "small," or avoiding doing anything at all. I quickly realized that I was very capable of hiking with my children, reading, and exercising if I scheduled these activities into my life. I have now become the poster child for the affirmation of: "Write it down." By scheduling these activities into my calendar, I was able to find an easy way to get them done and eliminate time as an excuse for not doing what is important to me.

As for the bigger goals, I have now been to Africa. I have also worked with a group of parents to build a school in my community. My family and I have traveled all over the world. These passions of mine turned out to be as attainable as those on the "easy" end of the spectrum, but they required more thought and planning. I have a Formula for Success that I use for achieving large goals that I will detail in the next chapter. It is something that I can teach you personally if you are interested in coming to work with me personally or at one of my live events.

When you look back at your life, you can see where you've been. When you look ahead in your life, do you know what you want it to look like? Can you see where you are going? What can you do to make your future conform to your ideas, instead of somebody else's idea of what it should be? Most of my clients indicate that there are lots of things on their list that are easily achievable and some are even very simple. It all begins with awareness.

Human beings require a discovery process that enables them to turn on their awareness and recognize how they use time as an excuse to keep themselves from experiencing everything they want to experience. I met a powerful woman recently who takes people all over the world on spiritual quests. In the course of our sharing, she told me that since she was eighteen years old that she'd always wanted to go to Spain, which was the birthplace of her father. Her father has now passed away, and she's fifty-three years old. Although she has taken many trips and seen so many things, she still has a piece missing in her heart. When we did this exercise together she said, "Gosh, if I just had time, I'd go to Spain."

I said, "Okay, I don't have a calculator here but fifty-three minus eighteen... it seems to me there might have been time to get to Spain, right?" All of us have times in our lives when we say, "Someday I'm going to..." But someday might not come. Most people never live to see someday. Again, this is where the three Ds come in. They provide an opportunity to take a hard look at your life. When you live on autopilot, you get so busy making a living that you forget that this is your life.

Recently, I was speaking with a friend of mine who had been diagnosed with fibromyalgia. She'd been a healthy, active, vibrant woman, but all of a sudden, she was in bed every day. She couldn't understand what was happening. Life happens while we are not looking. It woke her up to reality and the passage of time.

When I was younger, I was an entrepreneur in the restaurant business and worked seven days a week. People often asked me "Don't you feel like you don't have a life?" My answer was, "This is my life." Then life changed. I became pregnant with my son. All of a sudden, I didn't want to work seven days a week anymore. We sold everything and moved to the country. It was then that I realized you take yourself wherever you go. Although many factors contributed to the dissolution of my marriage, the bottom line was that I was fully responsible for not creating better communication and not being present to the gifts I had in my life.

Each and every one of us has opportunities to get a little clearer about our lives. If you're reading this, you have an opportunity to make a discovery for yourself. Take a look at what matters to you most. I have many of my clients do an exercise to discover where they are being stopped by their perception of a lack of time. Most people have a list of big dreams they believe are achievable with more time, but they also discover that there are small wishes that they can easily realize with a little focus. I believe most dreams, both big and small, are more achievable than we believe and getting clarity around our relationship to time goes a long way in assisting.

Ask yourself, "What am I not doing by saying I don't have time and money?" Did you make a discovery by looking at what you would be spending your time on if time and money weren't a problem? Understanding and acknowledging that should help you have an idea of what your core values are and what your goals should be—what really matters to you.

Take a moment and write down what really matters to you. For many people, the answers are home, family, relationships, spirituality, career, and finances. Can you imagine what it would be like if you could wake up every morning excited about your life? Do you want to continue to feel like you're going through the motions? Do you want to feel like you are passionate and excited every day? You know when you meet somebody who's living their true purpose. They are surrounded by a sort of glow, exuding passion and life. You also know when you meet somebody who's only going through the motions. It could be somebody who you run into in the grocery store. For example maybe you get the feeling from that guy behind the counter who is scanning groceries that he is not happy. You also get the feeling when you meet people who are turned on and fired up. Because they are being fulfilled and inspired in their own lives, they inspire us, too! That's the kind of life I want to show you how to live.

When I examined my relationship to time, I discovered that I was not taking care of myself through exercising. I decided to take action and began scheduling myself to take exercise classes. I realized that, without some outside structure, I wouldn't actually get it done. It was hard to commit initially, but once it became a habit, exercise became something that I look forward to.

Ideally, I exercise first thing in the morning, before I even start thinking about anything else. That's because when my brain kicks in, I'm much less likely to do it. I don't have to look pretty. I usually just put my hair into a ponytail and go. When I am near the ocean, I take advantage of the opportunity to start my day with a walk on the beach.

People seek me out to learn how to "get it all done." I do not have a magical formula, but beginning with this focus on time, was the first step for me in gaining momentum. We need to look at the big picture of life, and not be caught up in the details. We're all busy. We're spinning most of the time; that is, we are running on autopilot, always trying to get caught up and yet never realizing that precious time for the things we want is slipping away. By getting clear and focused on how you're spending your time, you will find opportunities for a better, more fulfilling life.

We sometimes feel like we want to resist structure. Once you have structure, time appears to become available for doing what you love and what is important to you. Writing it down and getting it in your schedule, scheduling time for what is important to you sounds too simple. We want to make it harder than that, but it really is fairly simple. It's a matter of what you're willing to commit to doing.

CHAPTER TWO

Overflowing Abundance

*"Being wealthy is not about having
money - it is about having options."*
Chris Rock

Have you ever heard of a man named Napoleon
Hill? His life is inspiring and can teach us
a lot about honoring the self, developing our
own personal value system, setting goals, and
learning how to create happiness and abundance
in our lives. Born in a one-room cabin in the

Appalachian coal mining region of southwestern Virginia in 1883, Hill went on to write one of the best-selling books of all time, *Think and Grow Rich*. He became personal friends with the steel magnate and great philanthropist Andrew Carnegie after the newspaper he wrote for assigned him to interview many rich and famous men. He became an advisor to two presidents, Woodrow Wilson and Franklin Delano Roosevelt. Hill believed that fear and selfishness were the two major obstacles to personal abundance and success. His idea of "definite major purpose" is part of the foundation of his book, and it begins with an examination of your values and pursuit of the knowledge of what you really want.

I would like to share with you my own discovery about money and abundance. Like many people, I grew up with the idea that money was scarce and that I would never have any. I viewed wealthy people as different or special. While I was growing up, my family always struggled financially and not having enough money was a constant stressor for us all.

When I was twenty, I took out a student loan for $2500 to study at Cambridge University in

England. This was the first student loan I ever took, and I was terrified. I had this idea that I would be a more valuable person if I "worked my way through college," and didn't take on any debt. Because I was usually working two jobs and attending classes in the evening, I might have been physically present, but I was rarely ever consciously present in my classes. No one in my family had ever been to college, and certainly not to Europe. When I learned of the opportunity to study abroad, I decided to go for it. I was nervous and excited and didn't know what to expect, but I knew that I might not have this opportunity again. My mother told me it was a big mistake because so much could go wrong. Again we didn't even know anyone who had traveled overseas, so it seemed like a pretty scary idea. I decided to take the loan anyway and go for it. I went to England, had an amazing few weeks studying at Cambridge, and then I ran out of money. I was flat broke. I called my mother and asked her to loan me $100. Her answer was that I had foolishly taken this trip against her advice, and she was not interested in bailing me out. She told me I was on my own, I was getting what I deserved and then she hung up the telephone.

I finished my time at the university in the dorm that was included in the trip, and then I had a few days left in England until my return plane flight. I knew I had a ticket home, so I would just have to figure out what to do in the meantime. I asked about changing the ticket, but I didn't have the cash or the credit for the change fee. For three days I slept in the airport in London. I didn't take a shower, had only a loaf of bread to eat, and nowhere else to go. Oddly enough, I didn't feel out of place. There were a lot of other kids there who were wearing jeans and carrying backpacks. Rather than feeling that I was in a dangerous place, I started to feel supported by complete strangers. Someone would come up to me and give me a newspaper. Then another person would come by and offer me a cup of coffee. I actually had a man say to me, "I haven't eaten this whole sandwich, would you like half of it?" The world that had appeared so scary and scarce to me started to shift.

When I returned to the United States, I stayed at a friend's house for a while. I had given up the lease on my apartment and the job I had counted on having when I returned was no longer available. There was something that shifted for me intellectually and emotionally when I realized that I was going to be alright even though I had none of the resources that I had grown to depend on. Being without money allowed me to see that money wasn't the object. I found another job, rented another apartment, and carried on with life, but I never saw or experienced money the same way again. The gift of being safe and sound without money, was a huge eye-opener for me. Many of my previous fears slipped away.

I believe this realization applies to all of us. We use money as a measure of our worth. For me, realizing that I was a valuable person without cash opened up a whole new world. Money became a tool to serve me and to help me get what I needed instead of the object of my work. My life began to feel more abundant and healthier on all levels, and money began to flow to me and through me with very little struggle.

I certainly have not always been financially successful. Like many people, I have made a lot of money and then lost it. When going through my divorce, I lost most of my financial worth. This was a great opportunity to look at what was working for me financially and what was not. I decided I needed some training and assistance to gain financial competence and decided to get some help from people who were wiser and more experienced than I. I quickly learned the habits I needed to adopt to begin the journey to financial stability.

How did I learn to let my money stay in my pocket, instead of going somewhere else? The most important factor, I quickly discovered, is believing you deserve to have wealth. So many of us have voices in our heads—old messages that are not even ours—telling us that we don't deserve to be comfortable financially. Many of us also struggle with old paradigms that tell us that there is something wrong with being wealthy. Like me, many of you grew up without an abundance of extra cash. Statistically this is where the majority of us stand. What I learned from my experiences, and from studying the experiences and behaviors of others, is that people who have money and people who do not have money have a big thing in common: they are all people! The huge difference is mind-set and habits. Each and every one of us can learn new mind-set distinctions and adopt new habits around money and wealth. We must first see ourselves as deserving beings and then realize that there is no lack of cash on the planet.

Adopting a new mind-set and habits requires clarification on how you're spending your time and what you truly value. In order to create and sustain a life that is fulfilling, dynamic, and purposeful, we must focus on our core values and learn to let go of the things that are not in alignment with them. When we are willing to do this, abundance shifts toward us. Abundance is what we are truly seeking—not cash. Money is simply a means to assist us with having the experiences we seek. Like most things, when you have money, it is no big deal. When you do not have it, it seems to be the most important thing in the world. Think about how this is true for most things in your life. When your relationship is good and things are going smoothly, there is not much to think about. When you have a relationship that is in trouble, it is all you can think about.

Now consider the logistics. People always want to know, "How do you make money?" Unfortunately, we keep looking for that magic bullet or magic wand. In reality, what works is not too surprising. In fact, you may have heard and read these distinctions many times in your life, but you must be in a frame of mind that calls you into action before you can implement the habits that will support you in being free from financial burdens.

First, you must learn to pay yourself first. If you are in business for yourself, it is easy to pay all of the other expenses first and leave yourself for last. This is not a path to wealth. If you are working for someone else and you are fortunate enough to bring home a steady paycheck, you must set aside funds for yourself (the form of savings is one option) before you pay your expenses. You've probably heard this before, and you've probably even read it, but try doing it. It will change your life and your relationship to money. This concept was revealed to me in reading Napoleon Hill's book, but the wisdom probably is much older. The challenge is not in the concept. The challenge is in the implementation.

A lot of people are afraid to perform this simple task for fear that a bill will come up that month when they least expect it. If your power bill went up $40 next month, would you still be able to pay it? For some of you that may be a tough question, and I understand. Many of us, myself included, have struggled so much financially, that a $40 increase in a bill would cause sleepless nights. However, I am proposing that paying that bill probably won't be impossible. You probably would still be able to eat and have a roof over your head, even if you had to pay the extra $40. So what if you shifted your perspective and took that money to pay yourself. If you set yourself up with a savings account that is attached to your checking account, the money is still easily accessible. If the need arises, you can still use it to pay that additional bill. But what if you don't need it to pay unforeseen bills. What if you began putting away $10 a week, $40 a month, and your money began to earn interest. The habit of paying yourself begins an amazing opportunity for financial growth, no matter what your initial dollar amount is. I have met many people who are financially independent who did not earn large incomes in their lives, but they did adopt good financial habits that supported them in achieving freedom.

Financial advisers will tell you that we need to save a full 10 percent. Now that abundance is flowing in my life, I actually put away much more than that, and I also make a practice of putting it in different places. When you get to that point, there is a whole structured philosophy about how to arrange your money, but you have to start somewhere. The practice of paying yourself is so powerful because it teaches you to value yourself, to initiate your own abundance, and to honor yourself. This is how you create your little nest egg that will grow bigger and bigger.

So how do you do it? I don't know what your actual numbers are, but let's say you have a paycheck coming in and you plan to start taking out 10 percent to pay yourself. After that, you must learn to live on 90 percent of your money by budgeting as if the 10 percent you put away doesn't exist. If you begin small, you can very quickly learn to live on even less than that 90 percent.

Finally there's that dirty word: budget. One of my personal financial mentors says that budgets don't work because people don't stick to them. If you can take the dirty part out of budget and understand that you must honor your time and your money, it will work.

There's something extremely important about putting away that first 10 percent. When you start, know that if you do have an emergency, or you have something come up, it's not like the money is gone. It's now in your savings account making money because it is compounding interest. No matter how small your investment is, the lesson and the benefits begin. It is a big step to learn to honor yourself. This is the secret that most people don't understand. We are still looking for the answer to be more complicated, but it is actually rather simple. If I can leave you with one gift, my request is that you try it. You have nothing to lose and everything to gain. You'll know whether or not it works. It doesn't require a tremendous amount of money, but it does require a commitment. It cannot work if you don't do it.

If it doesn't work for you, now what? You can always go back to the way it was before, but what if it does work for you? You now have a whole new way of thinking about your personal worth, a new way to honor yourself, and you've got some money in the bank. Later, when your finances become more secure, then you can save in several places. For example, I have money going into my childrens' college fund. I have money going into my husband's retirement account, and into my own retirement fund. I am saving other money for things I want now, things that are really fun, like traveling. Traveling is one of my great passions because I love to meet and be with people in other places in the world, and the more that I travel, the more that I find that we truly are all the same. Travel is a gift to myself, one of the things that aligns with my core values. Paying yourself makes realizing your dreams a reality. It is truly a crucial step in allowing real abundance to flow into your life.

After you adopt the habit of paying yourself, you must get rid of your consumer debt. This is a hard one for most of us, especially those of us who grew up in the United States with borrowing beyond our means as a habit. We are so fortunate to live in the United States, but I have friends in other countries that structure consumer debt differently. In the United States, we have for many, many years bought stuff on credit that we could not afford. We are currently experiencing a painful recession brought on in part by these habits.

The good news is that you can set yourself free if you take responsibility for your actions and adopt new habits that support you. I won't tell you that

I am so disciplined that I don't flip out the credit cards sometimes because I have and I do. I have several credit cards, and one of them is a business credit card that I pay off every month. I don't use my business card for things like jeans at Saks Fifth Avenue, as much as I'd like to. It is for business purposes only.

Business credit is directly related to business expense. However, there are subtle problems with business credit cards. As an entrepreneur, it is all too easy to justify personal expenses as business expenses. For example, I love to treat my employees to dinners and gifts; however, to make budgeting work, I treat that as a personal expense, not a business expense, since it doesn't bring in any profit. Whatever doesn't directly increase your profit or is not legitimately attached to your business belongs on your personal card. Your business expenses should live, breathe, and eat inside your business. If you have found yourself, like so many Americans, knee-deep in credit card debt, you are paying way too much interest. You must put a stop to this. No one can do it for you. One option, although it may seem painful at the time, is to start to eliminate your credit cards.

Literally take them one at a time and decide which one you are going to pay off first. It is amazing how quickly balances begin to diminish when the spending stops and you commit to pay more than the minimum balance each month. Begin with one – get it paid off – then put it away. Don't carry it in your wallet waiting to be used. If there is a purchase you need, the card will be there.

Once the first card is paid off, choose the second lucky card that will be cleared. Take the payments you were paying on card number one and now apply them to card number two – along with the usual payment you make to card number two. This takes tremendous discipline, but I know you can do it. The reward of no longer having this pressing debt hanging over your head will be worth it.

Having more than one credit card, all with balances going up at the same time, will gnaw at you, waking you up in the middle of the night to ask yourself how you are going to pay the bills. It's those little bills, the $100 here and $100 there, that eat up your time and your budget. One way to bring this issue into focus is to get very clear about where you're spending your money. Always look at your statement. Some credit cards will break down the percentages of what you've spent according to categories like restaurants, grocery stores, and so on. But you can do this for yourself. Try checking the percentages for a couple of months.

One of the ways you can make more money is to stop giving your money away by paying interest on credit cards. You gain absolutely nothing from that, and there's no long-term value in it. I am not proposing that you should have no credit cards, just that you choose to take back your power and really be responsible about your credit the same way you are responsible with cash. It is all too easy to think of credit cards as money that we own, but it is lent to us at a very high cost.

Credit cards do serve their purpose, once you take back your responsibility. Once I was traveling in San Diego and somebody ran into my rental car. The insurance provided by the credit card company was a great blessing. Likewise, online business often requires a credit card. In short, credit cards can be useful at times, but you must pay them off every month to avoid paying interest. Never use them like income because that's not what they are. Reigning in your credit card debt is my second major recommendation when developing a plan to achieve financial independence.

Another recommendation to help you reach your goal of financial independence has to do with cash flow. Adopting the idea of multiple streams of income is a large mindset shift for many of us who grew up in working class families. We only knew of getting a job, and if we were lucky, getting a good job. If you have only one source of income, maybe one job and a one paycheck, this can be a scary way to live. Many people have no choice about this, and many other people have no job at all. If you are able, I highly recommend that you find more than one income source so that if your primary source goes away or begins to dwindle, you will have another source. One of the reasons that I have learned to develop multiple businesses simultaneously is so that I can have more than one stream of income.

I know I have given you a lot to think about, but I really want to support you in getting a handle on financial self-sufficiency once and for all. We need to have a real look at self-denial. I promise you that you have the tools to make this happen for yourself, but if you are like most of us, the old voices and experiences may creep back in and you may sabotage your own progress. People fear structure and systems around finances, but the secret to success here is to embrace structure so that you can actually gain freedom. I know it sounds peculiar, but if you have ever adopted a habit around increase – a habit of working out to gain health, a habit of focus in an area of business to increase productivity, etc. – you will know what I mean. Structure around your spending will set you free. If you are worried about having to give up too much, focus on specifically what you are afraid of having to give up, like your shopping habit, smoking cigarettes, or eating out. Take an honest look and own that fear. For example, I love to eat out even though I also like to cook, and I like very good quality food. So if I have to give that up that might be scary, right?

This means that I must change that from something fearful into something that I can celebrate and reward myself with. Instead of eating out three days a week, I now think about eating out less. For example once every two weeks I go out and have a fabulous dinner, and rather than spending $20 three days a week, or $120 in two weeks, I go out for an amazing $60 dinner once every two weeks and get dressed up. I put makeup on, do my hair, and then drive into the city. I make it a big to-do, and I celebrate this reward of treating myself. If you go into this with the idea that now you're going to have to live like a monk and that you're going to be on a budget for the rest of your life and never have any fun, it won't work for you. I know I can't get excited about that. Like most people, I want to have a great time. So if I'm sitting here being smart about money, but then I think that to do so I can't have fun anymore, it's not going to stick. Changing that and making the fear into something that's actually fun and a reward will be worthwhile.

For those of you who are reading this book for support in your business, your answer to financial success is much of the same. I truly believe that professional growth and success follows personal growth. When considering a business expense, ask yourself, "Does my business really need this?" followed by "What is the return on this investment?" When somebody tries to sell me something for one of my businesses, my response is always, "Show me where that will make me money. I don't care if you're trying to sell me something for $1,000, or $20,000. Show me where the return is." If they can show me the value right up front, not in the distant future, then am I willing to consider their offer. It is always a surprise to me how many people are unable to do this. Business is about numbers. Period.

Deal with your business the same way that you take care of yourself and look for the payoff. Too often we spend before we look rather than focus and honor our hard-earned money. Honor the time, energy and labor that went into creating the revenue that you are reinvesting and then ask yourself if the funds would be better spent reducing debt. If the debt in your business is in any way related to you personally, get rid of it. If the debt is business-related, then before you take it on, ask about the return before you agree to invest. This extends to marketing or creation of new products or services, or web design. Before I spend money on anything, I ask myself, where is the return? Before I buy a company car, I ask myself which revenue stream is paying for it. You need to know how it's coming back before you buy it; if you honor that practice, you'll reduce your debt. Debt is only positive when you can see the return.

In our wine business, we often make large purchases for wine production. Contracts can range from $10,000 to $100,000. Before we sign the contract, we have to know what the return is going to be on that wine, and we have to figure in all of our costs, both seen and unforeseen, such as breakage, tasting samples for customers, promotional costs, overhead for the venue selling the wine, payroll, taxes, insurance, and so on. We have to know where the return is coming from before we write the check for the initial investment, and we want to see big margins, that is, a potentially big return, before we make any investment.

You've probably heard stories of people who won the lottery and within a very short time spent it all. In your own life perhaps you have experienced something like this too, a time perhaps when you've received some unexpected cash, won a settlement, received a large tax refund or inherited something, and suddenly you feel rich. Then a short time passes and you are feeling broke again. Maybe you couldn't understand why this happened or how the money seemed to disappear. Is there an underlying feeling or belief that you have about money that is preventing you from keeping it? When we get clear and focused on our beliefs around money and then adopt practices and habits that support us in attracting money and building wealth, it is much easier to maintain your financial worth. Having money and being comfortable financially becomes a natural experience instead of something we have to struggle around.

When we give up making money for money's sake, abundance flows to us and through us in a way that's empowering, inspiring, and, in my opinion, even a lot of fun!

Remember that honoring your time is the first piece of the puzzle, and the second piece is letting go of habits and attitudes that don't serve you. If you find yourself in a business or a personal situation that's not in alignment with your core value and your core goals, it's okay to say, "No." Similarly, if you find yourself in a professional situation with people who are not working with you in the same way or with the same passion that you work, maybe they're not in alignment with your values or your structure, and continuing with them might not be the highest and best use of your time and energy. Remember that there are many people who are in alignment with you and you will find them, or they will find you. You have to give yourself permission to let go of the people who don't share your goals. Understanding this and making it work in your life takes nurturing yourself, and it takes having other people teach and mentor you.

You also have to believe that you deserve an abundant life. I certainly did not always feel this way. At age twenty, I weighed only ninety-eight pounds. I was severely anorexic. When I look back at pictures of me, I find it shocking. I was a young woman who didn't believe that she deserved to be here or that anybody wanted me here. The reason I share that with you is that wherever you are currently, the voice inside you may not be your voice. It may be somebody else's voice from the past telling you that you're not good enough or that you don't deserve to have the life that you love, but it's not true. Each one of us is a child of God, and we all have the amazing potential to make a marvelous contribution to this planet and to each other. I encourage you to learn to support yourself, learn to let go of the things that are not in alignment with what is serving you, and begin to take those baby steps toward living a more abundant life.

One of the most important things that I now know is that money is a form of energy. When I started letting go of money for money's sake, my finances improved. Imagine sitting with me right now at a kitchen table with a big pile of cash on it. If I set the cash on fire, it might freak you out a little bit, but it would not change your life. Most of us attach so much meaning to money. We all desire to be comfortable financially and some us desire to have financial abundance, yet when real prosperity and abundance start flowing into your life, you must get clear about what it is underneath that you truly value.

When I host my three-day Passion, Purpose, and Profits Conference, attendees frequently want to know the secrets for getting rich. They want to find out immediately how to make a million dollars. I have to explain to them that if you don't understand the value of your time, experiences, and your contribution to the world, the money will quickly seep away. Money comes and goes; it flows to us and through us. It is simply a form of energy. It shows up in our lives in direct proportion to the number of people we are serving. When the outward flow starts to slow down, and you become comfortable financially, that is when you start getting very clear about why you want to have this money. Cash isn't the goal, even though we might think that it is.

Perhaps when you were growing up you thought having more money would prevent bad things from happening in your life. However, when you start making lots of money, it's the same game but with more zeroes. Now there's a mortgage, other bills, and bigger things you want, places where you want to travel, and things that you want to do. There are still contributions you want to make to those around you and the world, but now you can see bigger opportunities available. It becomes a matter of playing a bigger game, but, remember, you're still playing the same game, only with more zeroes.

Today my relationship to money is one of overflowing abundance, even though it didn't begin that way. I feel honored and grateful that there is always more than enough. Each and every one of us has a relationship to money. Discovering that relationship is not always easy because we're not always honest with ourselves. Coming clean with yourself and getting your values clear is a great place to begin. It is possible to live an abundant life without struggle and fear around hunger or homelessness. There's always enough. Each morning when I wake up, I give thanks for the abundance that I have in my life. I am grateful for my family, my health, and my community. I love where I live and who I live with. Starting my day with that focus attracts abundance into my life on multiple levels. I believe that the more you focus on something, the more of that "thing" you attract into your life. If you can give yourself a shift in perspective and focus from a place of gratitude and truly count your blessings, things begin to change. Try practicing gratitude and see how you feel and how life starts supporting you differently.

CHAPTER THREE

Walking in Faith

*"What plans would you have on your drawing board if
you knew you could not fail?"*
Reverend Robert Schuller

Praying is a personal subject. I was raised Southern
Baptist and although I loved many aspects of
my church community, I always questioned the
punitive side of my religion. As a young woman I
began studying different religions and fell in love
with Judaism. I loved the focus on family and

education, and I loved my perception (in Reform Judaism) that women should be treated with great respect. Judaism partly made such an impact on me because I lived in Miami, Florida, and the most successful people I met were Jewish. Not surprisingly, I decided to marry a Jewish man.

I intensely studied Judaism and Jewish culture for almost a full year before marrying my first husband. I still to this day love Judaism and am honored to have my children consider Judaism a part of their heritage. What didn't work for me was labeling myself as a devotee of one single religion. There were still facets of Christianity and Buddhism that felt authentic for me. When Scott and I got married, my daughter Erika was three years old. Erika told Scott that she believed I was half Jewish, half Christian, and half Buddha. This is a label I love.

In my own quest to know God and my Higher Source, I have discovered that, as a young woman, I only turned to prayer in very dark times. Often when I couldn't figure something out and felt like I was at my wit's end, I would ask God to assist me. Today I am blessed to have ongoing "conversations" with God.

Perhaps you have read, seen, or heard about Sharon Lechter and Greg S. Reid's book *Three Feet from Gold*. It tells the story of R.U. Darby and his uncle who were gold prospectors. After hitting a small seam of high-quality gold, they rejoiced and bought equipment to bring it out of the ground. They mined one full load, but then after that, much to their chagrin, they could find no more. They worked for weeks and months, maybe years, trying to find more, until they decided that they'd reached the end of a very small vein, and the end of their rope! Turning homeward in disgust, Darby sold their mining equipment to a junk dealer for only a few hundred dollars, much less than it was actually worth.

This junk man, however, turned out to be very wise indeed. Instead of reselling the equipment as junk, he sought the advice of an expert in the area of mining gold, a mining engineer. The engineer said that the Darbys had missed the seam, and he predicted that three feet from where they had stopped, they'd find the rest of the gold vein. When they dug, they picked it up again and, in fact, struck gold.

There are two morals to this inspiring story. One is that we need to seek the advice of mentors and experts and allow other people to guide us when we are entering an area in which we have no experience. The other is perseverance. So much is possible for us if we persevere through faith. In my own experience, amazing opportunities and gifts have presented themselves to me when I trusted my intuition and continued to follow a path in "blind faith," although my choices made little sense to the outside world.

I arrived at the life I live today through focus, perseverance, and faith. To live a life of ease and grace, you often have to grow and learn for a long time. My journey to the life of abundance that I am blessed with today did not happen overnight. There was an evolution that took place bringing me from a state of constant struggle to a place where life flows with ease and grace. I had a lot to learn and a lot to release. Although I no longer live with daily pain and struggle, I do still need to be reminded to accept and allow life to flow through me. Faith has been the strongest factor that has carried me through the darkest times.

When I have persevered through faith, loved myself, and recognized that I was good enough, the Universe began to bring people into my life to support me in sharing my message. I quickly realized that this support was unconditional and that I was not alone, which led to a paradigm shift in my life. Now, instead of seeing myself in competition with others in both my personal life and in my business, I am presented with collaboration opportunities on an ongoing basis. It is up to me to choose to embrace these opportunities, and when I do, I find that there is more available for me through collaboration than I could ever create or experience on my own.

Today I feel a new energy when I'm out in the world traveling and working with people that appears to be a reflection of my own personal adventure and journey. I believe that allowing The Universe to provide for us, understanding that there's more than enough for all, and feeling the support and the love of the people around us brings immeasurable success to our lives. Being strong and allowing these gifts to come to us by staying clear and focused and by not getting distracted by the inevitable tough times, carries us into a stream of peace and fulfillment. This is what I mean when I speak about walking in faith. When it feels like we are faced with people saying it can't be done, and we trust our intuition anyway, knowing that we are in our purpose, we come into our own. It's a combination of allowing and staying focused that brings wonderful things to each and every one of us.

I wish that our experience was one of growing pleasures instead of growing pains. For some reason we learn by facing challenges and by overcoming adversity. The hardest experiences we face are often the most rewarding growth opportunities when we reflect on what we have learned.

We all imagine perseverance as being engaged in a continuous struggle. But it doesn't have to be and shouldn't be the same as struggling. There's a place for each and every one of us where we can persevere without struggling, a place where we find focused action, moving continually toward our goal, without having to try so hard.

I heard something once in a training session being given by a man who was a Neuro-Linguistic Programming practitioner. He said, "I'm confused; I must be learning." This statement not only made great sense to me at the time, but it has stayed with me for years. If my brain is creating new pathways and I feel confused, I choose to embrace this feeling rather than allowing it to overwhelm me. I now embrace not knowing. What felt confusing for me in the past now feels like an opportunity to slow down so I can enjoy learning something new.

Chapter Four

Embracing Synchronicity

"Luck is a matter of preparation meeting opportunity"
Oprah Winfrey

Have you ever met someone and wondered why they were so lucky? More importantly, do you feel like an unlucky person yourself? If we grow up thinking of luck as something that we are not entitled to or something that doesn't exist, it doesn't appear for us. I don't believe much in luck. I do believe in our ability as human beings to recognize synchronicity. Webster defines synchronicity as the simultaneous occurrence of events that appear significantly related but have no discernible causal connection. How often have events appeared to be happening for you, but you chose not to pay attention to them or give them credence because they didn't make sense?

I believe successful people have a way of viewing the world that anyone can learn. Opportunities are all around us, yet our past programming leads us to believe that they are too good to be true, or that we need to be skeptical to protect ourselves. Seeing the synchronicity in things is like being aware and on alert for opportunities. The first step in becoming conscious is to realize where we are being unconscious.

People who are successful in business are masters at recognizing opportunities in the market place that need to be fulfilled. Most of the businesses that I've owned over the last twenty-plus years were ones that I had little or no experience in. They were ideas or opportunities that presented themselves to me and that I chose to embrace. First I would see an opportunity, then a niche, and then I would find another successful business in that industry and study it. No matter what you choose to do in business, chances are someone has done it, or something like it, before. Discover and study the distinctions that contribute to the success of a business in your industry, then model those distinctions.

When I first entered business and became an entrepreneur, I married a man who was a partner in a family-owned restaurant. We were truly self-employed people who worked seven days a week. When it came time for my husband and I to move on, we decided to open up a place of our own where we served breakfast and lunch five days a week located in an area surrounded by large businesses. That business was doing well and eventually gave birth to a catering company. The success of the first restaurant led us to create another one. Then we thought about how we wanted to raise our children. Working in this demanding business was not how I wanted to do it; rather, I wanted to move away from the metropolitan area, so my children could grow up in the country. We decided it was time to sell the restaurants and move to the country.

Each of my businesses tend to give birth to other businesses. For example, when Scott and I opened up the Art of Wine, a retail store in Sedona that sells wine and offers wine tasting, we sold $140,000 of clothing the first year. At the time, it blew us away that we could sell that much clothing out of a retail wine store. When we saw this opportunity, we launched a clothing store, named after our daughter, Erika Morgan, right next door. Making your businesses grow and thrive is largely a matter of recognizing synchronicity and being conscious of the gifts being brought into your life. If you focus on the gifts, and you pay attention to timing and connections, you will begin to see an infinite number of opportunities where none appeared before.

If you don't see such opportunities opening up, try to focus on the gifts around you. We are all learning to be more conscious, and there are gifts and great abundance around us all the time, whether we acknowledge it or not. Have you ever noticed that you get more of what you focus on? If you can turn your focus to the places where the flow is coming in, be it in business, love, health or other gifts, and choose to celebrate these gifts, you may be pleasantly surprised to see how these gifts grow.

CHAPTER FIVE

Real Connections

*"We are not put on this Earth to see through one
another. We are put on this Earth to see
one another through."*
Gloria Vanderbilt

When I was growing up, I felt few genuine human
connections. My parents lived in constant fear and
we were very isolated outside of our time spent
at school. It wasn't really a function of their
financial struggles, although I don't think that

helped matters. It was more a fear of being hurt or taken advantage of. I don't remember consciously wishing to be wealthy, but I do remember feeling that rich people were somehow different from us. When I saw someone whom I perceived was rich, I assumed that person was happy and had everything going for him or her. I didn't know much about people who were different. My family didn't have friends over, and extended family members rarely visited. When they tried to connect, they were quickly dismissed and invited to leave.

My parents' fears that everyone was out to get us were well ingrained in my brother and I. It was terrifyingly ironic that the "uncle," who was unrelated to us, but willing to care of us on the weekends, sexually molested me for more than six years. Needless to say, my perceptions were that my parents' beliefs were true and that it wasn't very safe to get too close to anyone.

When I was twenty-three, the insurance company I worked for offered me the opportunity to move to Texas and open a branch office. I had finished college and had not yet been accepted to law school, so I decided to give it a try. My relationships with others at this time started to shift. People in Texas are friendly. I was extremely surprised and taken aback when complete strangers greeted me at the grocery store or at the gas station. Initially, when someone would ask me how I was doing, I would put my head down and avoid the conversation. I was always prepared for them to be dangerous, or to start asking me for money. After several months of this, I began to realize how very lonely I was, so I decided to take a chance and respond when I was spoken to. At first it was terrifying, but slowly I began to get more comfortable. I made my first friendship with a girl who lived in the apartment below mine. I decided this was going so well, that I was probably safe to actually smile and allow myself to engage in brief conversations with the people I met at work. A part of me that I had never recognized began to blossom.

I decided that if it was OK to speak with other people, perhaps I could do a little experiment. I had never received compliments or acknowledgment in my home as a child, but I had received recognition from employers and teachers, and I knew enough to know how wonderful it felt. I began to experiment with recognizing the goodness in others and offering them my compliments. Even though this felt strange at first, I recognized something special in the people around me and loved to see how they lit up when I gave them compliments. I didn't go overboard, and I managed to keep my observations appropriate so I wouldn't be inauthentic. Almost miraculously, the world began opening up and I began to feel lighter and somehow supported. Coworkers and others I came into contact with on a day-to-day basis could not seem to do enough for me. It was more than a little mind blowing for a girl who grew up in survival mode and constant fear.

This quiet personal experiment has become a way of life for me today. I am constantly honored by the people I meet in the world and am blessed to share an intimate relatedness with complete strangers on a regular basis. I was at first surprised and uncertain about why I would be speaking to people on planes and all of a sudden they would begin to share with me their most personal stories. What I have come to realize by writing my story is that I am available to people in a way that most people do not experience in their day-to-day lives. Many people are never listened to because we so often get so caught up in our lives and so busy earning money, we forget about our real lives. Likewise, we get into routines and habits and take the people around us for granted. When a complete stranger shares with me his or her deep, full story, I feel deeply moved and honored to listen. When I began personally mentoring clients, I discovered (because I asked) that almost all of them felt unheard. Again, something so simple can make such a profound difference.

I do believe that I have been open to connections because I was blessed with one person in my childhood who really heard me. When my brother and I were very young, we had a babysitter named Barbara Wiesinger, and she is one of the most generous, amazing women I've ever met in my life. She provided my brother and I with a safe, stable place to stay, when the rest of the world felt very scary. Whether or not my parents could pay her, we were always welcome in her home. I never realized how much she meant to us when we were small, but I have come to know as an adult that she was the role model who taught me about compassion and the best of humanity.

Not long ago my husband and I were passing through Miami, on our way to the Caribbean and

Scott suggested that we give Barbara a call. We got lucky and she was home. I used the occasion to tell her that one of the most important values that I have in my life is the opportunity to make a contribution, and that really came from being with her and watching how she always contributed to others. I thanked her again for always offering me a safe place for me during my childhood.

Over the years, Barbara has cared for many children and opened her home to hundreds of them, showing them all love. She was the person I turned to when I was in need, and hers was a safe place to be. On this visit she told me that I called her from the hospital when I was in labor, giving birth to my son, almost twenty years ago. To this day, I have no recollection of making that telephone call. She told me, "You called me and told me how much you love and appreciate me." Although I did not necessarily have the relationship that I wanted in my family of origin, I was blessed to have this woman in my life. She truly is and has been a role model for me for healthy connections and unconditional love.

The rewards of being connected with others are too measurable for me to address in this short book. If you have felt, like I did, that the world was not necessarily a friendly place, I encourage you to try on my personal experiment and allow yourself to be available. Most of the people that I meet who live in isolation are beautiful beings who just haven't been given the tools for connecting. The world is so much richer when you have another being to share your experiences with. I am not proposing a huge change, just small steps in giving and receiving companionship and communication.

For those of you who are seeking business distinctions from this book, please remember that "no man (or woman) is an island." The only way to grow your abundance and your productivity in life and in business is through collaboration and partnership. By reaching out and being open to new communications, you may just meet the ideal person to support you and your new adventures.

Chapter Six

Use Others' Wisdom

"The greatest thing is, at any moment, to be willing to give up who we are in order to become all that we can become."
Max De Pree

At this point you know that where I came from was not to determine where I am today. When I was twenty years old I worked not only as a receptionist in a law firm but also as a waitress, and I went to college in the evenings. It was a very unconscious time in my life. I was basically numb. I worked very hard and was desperate for any recognition. I told myself that I was so thin because I was working so hard. In reality, I was severely anorexic, weighing ninety-eight pounds on my twenty-first birthday. My desperate state made me an easy target. I dated a man who alternated between living with me and being the entire focus of my life to breaking up with me—usually in a fit of rage—and beating me soundly before he would take off and live with another woman. I would be devastated and feel like I was falling apart until he would call and come back and the cycle began again. This rollercoaster carried on for more than two years during which time I would rarely eat or sleep.

My life changed because of the wisdom of others. I literally could not see myself or my situation objectively. One day a woman I worked with, Estrella, confronted me at work. She came up to my desk and said, "Laura, it doesn't have to be this way." I was terrified that I had done something wrong in the office, but she pulled me outside and explained to me that she had seen the bruises on my face more than once. I assured her that it was no big deal, and that John and I had just had a fight. She listened to my excuses then gently and generously shared with me that she had once been in a similar situation of domestic violence. She shared with me that there was a whole different world available for me if I would have the courage to be open minded. She suggested that I allow her to connect me with a counselor who could help me. In my current state, I was always in trouble financially, so I couldn't fathom how I was going to afford help. Estrella, which means "star" in Spanish, was truly an angel in my life. Through her guidance, I connected with a wonderful therapist, Tom Norris, who provided a safe place for me to shift my perspectives. He showed me that I could be strong and healthy and choose a different path from the one I was on.

Tom became the first of many people who compassionately mentored me over the next twenty years. As I've grown in my confidence and clarity of purpose, mentors have come into my life like magnets. Part of this is my ability to embrace synchronicity, but part of it, I believe, is a gift from the Divine. I believe mentors and opportunities present themselves to us when we are ready to receive them. We must be conscious enough to pay attention to what's working and what's not working in my life, and letting go of the things that are not working. You can choose to do this as well.

So many of us struggle with things that are not in our best interest to concern ourselves with. I always say that I am so grateful now that I don't have to invent the wheel. Someone did it a long time ago. I can now focus on the things that I am good at and work with opportunities as they present themselves to me, rather than constantly living under a self-imposed pressure that I have to do everything myself or that I am responsible for everyone else's business.

I have been fortunate to achieve success in several different business arenas. I attribute these successes primarily to seeking out people who have been successful in these arenas and modeling their behaviors. For example, if I want to be successful in the real estate business, all I have to do is educate myself on what is working and who is enjoying success in that industry. This strategy has worked for me in hospitality, real estate, viniculture, retail businesses, service businesses, consulting, speaking, producing events, fundraising, and more. Wherever you are or want to go, chances are someone has gone before you and made a success of it. Reach out to them and let them share with you their lessons.

If we can learn to let go of the fears that hold us back—the fear that we are not good enough, the fear that we don't know enough, the fear that others won't care about our problems—, and we can learn to let go and use the wisdom of those who have gone before us, our journey can be so much easier. Our load is much lighter when we focus on our gifts, rather than feeling like we have to carry the weight of the world on our shoulders.

Let others support you. One of the greatest gifts you can give a successful person is to ask for his or her advice. Most of the people that I meet who are truly successful, not just in one area of their lives but on multiple levels, are eager to pay their success forward. It feels great when you achieve a certain level of success and you are able to share your experiences with another person so that they can reach their success that much faster.

Do you know the difference between a smart person and a wise person? A smart person learns from her or his mistakes. A wise person learns from the mistakes of others. Simply said, choose to be a wise person

CHAPTER SEVEN

Put Your Own Spin on the Wheel

"Each individual brings something of unrepeatable dignity and goodness into the world, no matter who they are or where they come from."
Dr. Jeffrey Rediger

I would like to leave you with the request that you find time for play in your life. I spent most of my youth, twenties, and early thirties, working so hard to gain approval and acceptance that I never gave myself permission to play. To be fair with myself, I am not sure I knew how to play. It is a sad memory for me that I do not recall hearing my mother laugh when I was a child. That is not a legacy I wanted for my own children.

When I married Scott, he had such a zest for life. I thought he was a party animal and there was no way we could ever have anything in common. Slowly, over the years, in between working and building and studying, he would pull me away and want to play. It might be going out with friends or playing cards. He supported me in my quest to travel the world, and even when it didn't seem like we could afford to go on a vacation, we would still make time to travel.

Many of my clients do not believe that they can own and operate successful businesses and still find time to play. I encourage them to discover their core values through a process I teach called "The Circle of Life." Once we discover their core values and I support them in designing a structure to support those values, while still maintaining effective business systems to ensure their financial success, they are always amazed to find that there is time for both personal and professional success.

Each of us brings our own unique gifts to the planet. I encourage you to embrace a path that allows you to express those unique gifts with others while experiencing all the joys that a full, connected life can provide you with.

CHAPTER EIGHT

Parting Words

*"If you want to live a life you love, start
loving the life you live."*
Laura Gisborne

True abundance in your life begins with gratitude.
If you think that it's tough and that you're
struggling, the best advice that I can offer you is to
get out of your own way and start looking outside
of yourself. Many people all over the United States
are homeless, and seeing people in these situations

makes it a little easier to realize all the blessings you have. In order to thrive and receive the fullest blessings in our own lives, we need to recognize the people that love us.

I believe that we are all children of God. I believe we are all here with a purpose, but we hold ourselves back because we're afraid. We're afraid that we're not enough. We're afraid that nobody cares. We're afraid it's not going to be right. What changes the world, however, is action: getting out there, taking the initiative, making mistakes, learning, and growing. We all have that ability to get out there and do it, but we're afraid.

Revisiting the stories I have shared with you makes me realize that living a life that you love takes practice. It is all too easy to slip into the mind-set and patterns of my childhood, if I don't stay clear and present to the blessings and the good things in my everyday experiences. One of the daily practices that helps keep me on track is starting each day with a gratitude prayer. I am not much of a morning person, and I like to wake up slowly. Once my husband gets out of bed, I lay there for a while and give thanks for all of the things I am grateful for that day. The first things usually come fairly easily—for my health, my children, my husband, my beautiful home, my community, my friends, the opportunity to do my work in the world and feel purposeful. Then I give myself a few minutes to go a little deeper and give thanks for the blessings I may not realize on the surface, such as being born in America where I have such freedom of choices, being born a woman, and having the life experiences that have taught me so much—especially the painful ones. This practice starts my day in a way that has me getting out of bed in the mindset that I am the luckiest woman in the world. If you don't enjoy mornings, try this and see how it feels. It is a simple practice that goes a long way for me.

In closing I would like to share with you the words that hang above my desk so that I see them every day.

Watch your thoughts—
They become your words.

Watch your words—
They become your actions.

Watch your actions—
They become your habits.

Watch your habits—
They become your character.

Watch your character—
It becomes your destiny.

Frank Outlaw

My parting wish for you…

Salud, Dinero y Amor y tiempo para disfrutarlo.

Roughly translated, I wish for you Health, Wealth and Love and the time to enjoy them.

All my Best,

Laura

For information on how to work with Laura, please visit www.Lauragisborne.com.

Made in the USA
San Bernardino, CA
28 July 2014